AD LIMINA APOSTOLORUM

AD LIMINA APOSTOLORUM

An Appraisal of Vatican II

BY KARL BARTH

Translated by Keith R. Crim

JOHN KNOX PRESS
Richmond, Virginia

Translated from the German by Keith R. Crim, with the permission of EVZ-Verlag, Zürich (©️ 1967). The Appendix, "Thoughts on the Second Vatican Council" by Karl Barth, is from *The Ecumenical Review*, Vol. XV, July 1963, No. 4, pp. 357-367. Reprinted by permission of the author and *The Ecumenical Review*.

CONTENTS

TRANSLATOR'S NOTE

All references to *The Documents of Vatican II* are to the paperback volume edited by Walter M. Abbott, S.J., published by Guild Press, America Press, and Association Press, New York, 1966, and used by permission of Guild Press. Most of the documents are divided into chapters, which are always designated by Roman numerals. The basic division of the documents, however, is into sections numbered consecutively with Arabic numerals throughout each separate constitution, decree, or declaration. Some of these sections contain more than one paragraph. Although these are not numbered in the Documents themselves, Prof. Barth often identifies them for ease of reference. Thus in the questions for clarification on the Constitution on the Sacred Liturgy, for example, 35, 1-2 refers to the first two paragraphs of the section numbered 35, and 9-52 refers to sections 9 through 52 of this Constitution.

References to earlier Councils are to Denzinger, Henrici, *Enchiridion Symbolorum* (Herder: Freiburg, Breisgau, thirtieth edition, 1955). An English edition was published as *The Church Teaches* (St. Louis, Mo.: B. Herder Book Co., 1955).

ACCOUNT
OF THE
TRIP TO ROME

ACCOUNT OF THE TRIP TO ROME

It has been about two and a half years since I received an indirect and unofficial inquiry from the well-known Secretariat for Christian Unity in Rome. Would it please me to have a personal invitation to the final two sessions of the Second Vatican Council as an "observer"? It would certainly have pleased me, but the inquiry reached me, if I remember correctly, during one of my then very frequent stays in the hospital, and so, prevented by a higher power, I was forced to forgo the opportunity.

Then in May 1966 the plan formed in my mind (perhaps under the stimulus of the magnificent Catholic church music of Mozart which I—and others as well—enjoyed shortly before my eightieth birthday) of laying aside for a while my autobiography, on which I had been at work during the previous winter, and turning once more to present-day theological concerns. Not that I wanted to take part in the discussions of the idiotic "God is dead" movement, which on both sides of the Atlantic was showing itself to be the ultimate and fairest fruit of the glorious existential theology; and I had even less desire to take part in the just as idiotic "Confessional Movement" which some persons, who intellectually and spiritually were neither qualified nor called, felt they had to rush into in order to oppose those others. Definitely not! For my part, even while I was sick, I had—out of my long-term interest in the much more pressingly rele-

vant and objectively more significant problem of Roman
Catholicism—read all the news and German texts of the
documents of the Council that reached me, besides reading Goethe, Jeremias Gotthelf, Gottfried Keller, and
other good writers. And then, since my spirits were beginning to revive through the goodness of God and the
skill of my doctors, I wrote a letter to Rome. Were they
inclined to receive me, as it were, *post festum*, so that I
could acquire firsthand information? It would be a
purely private matter of instructing me in the way the
decisions of the Council were understood and explained
in the immediate vicinity of the center of the Catholic
Church. On this side of the Alps, present-day Catholic
theology was not unknown to me through its literature
and to some extent through its representatives. Now I
wanted to become acquainted with it where it had long
been operating, and from where, with conflicting and
interrelated tendencies, it had now adopted for itself new
standards and directions. The answer from Rome was
very friendly and cordial, as I had been sure it would be.
The Secretariat for Christian Unity, to which I want to
express my especial thanks, did everything needed to
open the way for me to meet a great number of persons
and groups who are characteristic of the situation in
Rome since the Council.

Now, anyone who really wants to receive information
must first of all be informed to some extent already. So in
the course of the summer I undertook the serious study
of the sixteen Latin texts worked out by the Council and
of at least some of the wealth of material dealing with
the Council. As a result, during my conversations in
Rome some of my interlocutors praised me for having
examined the texts at least as closely as they had, and in

some details more closely. I worked out a total of ten sets of questions on the pronouncements of the Council that seemed to me the most important—one general set of questions and nine double sets: Questions for Clarification and Critical Questions. Naturally I dealt first of all with the four "Constitutions," and then also with three of the nine "Decrees" and two of the "Declarations." It was not that I was not interested in the other seven documents—e.g., the decree on the training of priests—but I could not count on more than five working days in Rome since I would be there over a Sunday. Even so, in the materials I had selected and worked over I was unable in Rome to complete the discussions of the very important Decree on the Missionary Activity of the Church.

Armed with these preparations I made my pilgrimage to the threshold of the Apostles September 22-29. Since my physical condition was still not perfect but in need (then as now) of some attention and care, I was accompanied by my good wife and (as was doubly appropriate) my Catholic friend and physician Dr. Alfred Briellmann, M.D.; but during that week's time I caused them no serious concern. Both of them participated as alert observers in all the visits and encounters which I enjoyed while there. From the other side we were guided, introduced, instructed, and, from time to time, also entertained in a more worldly manner by Bishop Willebrands, the representative of Cardinal Bea in the Secretariat for Christian Unity, by the thoroughly Swiss Fr. Magnus Löhrer from Einsiedeln (now professor in the Benedictine College of San Anselmo in Rome), and occasionally by Msgr. Salzmann from Oberwallis. In earlier years I had been in Rome several times, but never had I enjoyed it as much—in the best sense of the word—as this time.

Certainly one reason for this was that now I was not merely a curious tourist (we did a lot of sightseeing in Rome and the vicinity) but that I had work to do.

The discussions were held in part in the rooms of the Secretariat for Christian Unity and in part in the residences of the various persons and groups whom I wanted to hear and who were interested in my visit.*

The conversations were conducted in the following manner. Mimeographed copies of two or three of my sets of questions chosen for the particular occasion were placed in the hands of the Catholic theologians who were taking part. I explained the questions to them, if necessary, and then listened to their answers. This procedure often took up to three hours. As a rule the discussions were held in French. On both sides the atmosphere in which this took place was always characterized by brotherly trust, frankness, and relevance. If I encountered points that were hard, or points that were too soft, I took great care not to press further but hurried on to the next point. I had certainly not gone there to quarrel.

As I recall them, the most lively of these discussions (without meaning to slight the various Dominicans, Benedictines, Franciscans, and other scholars with whom I also discussed) were those with the Jesuits on the battlements of their Gregoriana, where I was seated so as to enjoy the splendid autumn weather, looking directly at the dome of St. Peter's all the while, and thus in the flow of our discussions never able to forget where I was. I

---

* Quite some time after my return from Basel I discovered, in a sensational article in the *Frankfurter Allgemeine Zeitung* which was picked up by various Swiss newspapers, that there was one place in Rome, the Lateran University, where they slyly but firmly refused to receive me. I will not repeat here the scurrilous details with which the article was dressed up. I know from the most reliable sources that these details were the invention of the newspaperman in question.

was particularly impressed by a Spanish Jesuit who was an extremely helpful partner in dialogue. In the "Holy Office," where not many "separated brethren" come and go, I was instructed by Cardinal Ottaviani and Archbishop Parente concerning the more conservative direction and orientation of the Council. I also visited the home of Cardinal Bea on the Via Aurelia, the road that led to the northwest from ancient Rome. He is well known and rightly honored in the non-Roman ecumenical movement, and I found him to be an undeniably good man in the service of an undeniably good cause, which, it must be admitted, he represents with a rather conventional theology. This is preferable to the cases where some others use a more modern theology to present a less worthy cause! Augustin Bea is from the Black Forest, and a clock that obviously came from there accompanied our conversations with its ticking, occasionally interrupted by the call of the cuckoo.

The Sunday we were in Rome we attended Mass in the Church of St. Louis, where the sermons and prayers are in French. At the door we received a courteous welcome from the officiating priest and found, contrary to some gloomy predictions with which I was started on my journey, that the liturgical reforms had been definitely put into practice in Rome, at least in this church. Two months earlier I had seen them in effect in a remote mountain village in Wallis. And with all our Catholic contacts, we naturally did not fail to spend a few hours among our Waldensian brethren. Bishop Willebrands accompanied us there also. We met, among others, a lady from Basel. It was here that Oscar Cullmann regularly had his residence during the years when the Council was in session.

On the final day of our stay we had the opportunity to

participate in the International Congress of Theologians who were then gathered in Rome from all parts of the globe. In the lobby of the meeting hall we were surprised by a united choir of young Protestants and Catholics from Wettingen in Aargau, who welcomed us there in the center of Rome with Nr. 73 from our hymnal, "All Morgen ist ganz frisch und neu des Herren Gnad und grosse Treu" ("The Lord's grace and faithfulness are fresh and new every morning"). In the auditorium, which was decorated with a larger than life picture of the Pope (perhaps designed as a warning to overly bold innovators), I was greeted by applause, honored by a respectful greeting, personally introduced together with the cardinals who were present (as if I were one of them, except that I lacked the red hat), and then seated in an armchair a little removed from them, but on the same level. We heard a lecture by Karl Rahner on the presence of Jesus Christ in the Eucharist, in which only the frequent use of the modern Latin word "existentialis" sounded rather queer to me, and a discussion led by Professor Semmelroth. How I envied the Catholic theologians their skill, developed from youth on, in using Latin in their lectures and discussions as if it were the mother tongue of them all. If there is to be meaningful progress in the famous "dialogue" among the churches we will certainly have to train our successors in this skill. After this thought-provoking encounter we met in the Secretariat for Unity and held a private conversation with our colleagues Rahner, Ratzinger, and Semmelroth, during which I asked them to let me hear their somewhat divergent views on Mariology.

The high point of our days in Rome, for drama if not for content, was naturally our reception in the innermost sanctuary of the Roman Catholic Church. Although in the Lateran—more papal than the Pope—they ignored me, as I said above, we received a friendly invitation to visit the "Holy Father"—as Catholics call him—in the Vatican. The proverb "Who is so smart as not to find his master in the Vatican" ran through my head, but I should add at once that no one there made the slightest attempt to master me and that I count the full hour which Pope Paul VI gave me as among the most pleasant memories of our week. Led by Bishop Willebrands through a whole row of antechambers, past the Swiss guards with their glittering halberds, we came at last to the Pope's study where "Sa Sainteté" (here, too, we spoke French) met me at the door, literally with outstretched arms. The Pope seemed to be to some degree informed about my previous activities, for he began with some words of praise and then hinted that it is no easy task to bear the keys of Peter. But since the Lord had entrusted them to him, he was willing to bear the burden. I then, modest as I am, was bold enough to present him with some of the questions I had brought with me. For example, those dealing with my theological status as one of the *"fratres sejuncti,"* as we are always called in the documents of the Council. I asked whether he agreed with what I had been told elsewhere in Rome, that in this formula the stress was on the word *"fratres."* He seemed to agree. We did not pass over even the difficult point of Mariology. The Pope had heard that I preferred Joseph, the foster father of Jesus, as the prototype of the nature and function of the church, to the "handmaiden of the Lord" who was subsequently elevated to the position of Queen of Heaven. He assured me he would pray for me, that in my advanced age I would be given deeper insight into this problem.

But here, too, everything passed pleasantly, and the

hour flew by. It ended by my presenting to the Pope four of my smaller books (hauled out of an old but still usable briefcase which had accompanied me at the Synod of Barmen in 1934) in French and Spanish translations. He observed with a smile that it would have been troublesome for me to have brought him my *Church Dogmatics* in the same manner, the extent of which at least did not seem unknown to him. For his part he gave us each a medal from the Council and gave me a magnificent facsimile edition of the text of the Gospels of the Codex Vaticanus, the sight of which will give pleasure to my grandchildren and great-grandchildren. The way in which Paul VI received us and took leave of us was dignified and human in the highest sense. He impressed me as an intelligent and, in his own way, a definitely humble, pious person. During that hour there was no moment when I was forced to think of the title he bears of *Pontifex Maximus*. On our side it should be clearly noted that he did not call himself "Vicar of Christ" in any of the documents of the Council but simply, "Bishop, servant of the servants of God." If I on my part had opportunity to wish him something, it would be a greater measure of "cheerful confidence" (*parrhesia*) in relation to those inner tensions in his church which in part made the Council necessary and in part are the result of the Council. But you would yourself have to be Pope in order to know how hard it must be, in the midst of already existing problems and those which have newly developed, to serve the cause of true freedom and that of necessary order, as Paul VI obviously seeks to do. One thing will make his name remembered in the history of the church and the world: his courageous and persistent commitment to peace among the nations, and especially in Vietnam. From his important post—as also from Geneva—the church has not been silent this time; it has not blessed any weapons.

And then, after visiting the graves of John XXIII and his predecessor Pius XII, we found ourselves under the bright Italian sky in St. Peter's Square, where in ancient, modern, and most recent times so many remarkable events have taken place.

On September 29 we left the threshold of the Apostles behind, journeyed toward the Gotthard Pass, and reached again our household gods, rather tired but intact.

As a result of the trip I gained a close acquaintance with a church and a theology which have begun a movement, the results of which are incalculable and slow but clearly genuine and irreversible. In looking at it we can only wish that we had something comparable, if it could avoid a repetition of at least the worst mistakes we have made since the sixteenth century. I would be happy to see the words "Protestant" and "Protestantism" disappear from our vocabulary—and along with them the backwoods article of exception in our Swiss Constitution. The Pope is not the Antichrist! The apparatus of all the anathemas directed at us by the Council of Trent is now to be found, with all sorts of other old weaponry, only in Denzinger. *Ultra montes* I met so many Christians with whom I could not only speak candidly and seriously, but also join in hearty laughter, that I could not think without pain of certain dwarfs in our own theological backyard. Any optimism about the future is automatically excluded. But calm, brotherly hope is called for, together with a willingness in the meanwhile to conduct in both great and small affairs a thorough housecleaning of our own. "Conversions" from us to the Roman Catholic Church or from there to one of our churches have as such no significance (*peccatur intra muros et extra!*).

They can have significance only if they are in the form of a conscientiously necessary "conversion"—not to another church, but to Jesus Christ, the Lord of the one, holy, catholic and apostolic church. Basically both here and there it can only be a matter of each one heeding in his place in his own church the call to faith in the one Lord, and to his service.

The rest of this little book consists, first of all, of the questions which I took to Rome and asked there. It is obvious that when I formulated them I did not have in mind an evaluation of all the documents of the Council, and that after my journey to Rome I would formulate them a little differently from before. Because from the beginning I assured the Secretariat for Unity of my strict discretion, the reader will find here nothing of the answers (sometimes, lack of answers) which my questions received in Rome.

Also I have added a short essay which I later contributed, in response to a request from Yves Congar, O.P., who had been in Rome at the same time, for a gathering he organized in Strasbourg to discuss the Constitution on Divine Revelation. In addition, there is a private letter to a German Catholic theologian who had sent me his unpublished lecture on Mariology for my views and reactions. Anxious souls on our side may here at last see that I returned from Rome just as stubbornly evangelical—I would really rather say, evangelical-catholic—as before.

I will discuss the Constitution *Dei Verbum* here in the course of the winter semester 1966-67 in my well-known colloquium at the school of theology.

QUESTIONS
ASKED IN ROME

GENERAL QUESTIONS

1. Do the actions of the Council have a definite central point of emphasis?

2. Was Vatican II a reforming council? (This is sometimes disputed.)

3. What does *aggiornamento* mean? "Accommodation" to what?

4. Was the main concern a renewal of the Church's theoretical and practical understanding of itself in the light of the revelation on which it is founded, or a renewal of her thinking, speaking, and acting today in the light of the modern world?

5. If both, in the interests of the pastoral task, which was it primarily?

6. On which of these two types of renewal will the stress be placed in the period after the Council?

7. Are the adherents of the "progressive" majority of the Council, who opt for the latter, aware of the danger that this might result in an undesired repetition of the errors committed in modern Protestantism?

CONSTITUTION ON THE SACRED LITURGY

1. Is it a correct understanding of the Council to assume that it was concerned here in a decisive way with the following practical innovations or new beginnings:

(a) greater attention to Holy Scripture (35, 1-2; 51)

(b) integration of the sermon into the worship of the Mass (9-52)

(c) simplicity, brevity, and intelligibility of the rites (34)

(d) widest possible use of the vernacular (36; 54; 63; 78; 101)

(e) adaptation to the various cultures and their customs (40)

(f) conscious and active participation of all in the entire liturgy (19; 48)—even in the sacrifice (48)?

2. Is it the case, as was stated by the German-speaking bishops in their declaration of December 4, 1963, that the meaning of all these practical postulates is "the inner renewal of the *ecclesia viva catholica*"?

3. Can we find among the postulates cited one or more which had central meaning and urgency in the thought of the Council?

II. CRITICAL QUESTIONS

1. What does it mean to say that through the liturgy "the work of our redemption is exercised" (2; 6, etc.)? Would it not be more appropriate to speak of a central

answer of God's people, or of the testimony which they are to bear?

2. Is Christ present in the Mass only "in the person of His minister" and in the two elements of the Eucharist (7, 1) when it is stated in 48 that the faithful, together with the priest, offer the "Immaculate Victim" ("not only through the hands of the priest, but *also with him*")?

3. What is the basis for treating "communion under both kinds" (except for that of the priest) as an extraordinary case (55)? Is the reference to the Council of Trent adequate?

4. Had the eucharistic celebration already taken on in the New Testament church the primary significance ascribed to it here and in the other documents of Vatican II?

DOGMATIC CONSTITUTION
ON THE CHURCH

1. In the relationship of chapters I and II, is the "Body of Christ" subordinated to the "People of God," or vice versa?

2. According to 14-15, what are the "separated brethren"? Of what does the "entirety" of the faith which is reserved to the Roman Catholic Church consist?

3. Did Paul belong to the "college" of the apostles, over which Peter presided (19-26)?

4. Are only the pope, bishops, priests, and deacons "partakers of the function of Christ" (28)? If so, then the laity (30-42) are not a part of the hierarchy, are they? But why not, since they share in all the three offices of Christ, and in the apostolate of the church?

5. Are the predicates of Mary—Advocate, Auxiliatrix, Adjutrix, and Mediatrix (62)—to be understood only in the context of pious invocation? (Thus Ratzinger.) If so, is this interpretation to be extended to all Mariology (e.g., immaculate conception and assumption)?

1. Wherein lies the difference between Christ as Lord, King, and Judge and his church? Are only the laity his witnesses in the world? Are the hierarchy more than that? Is not the whole church a witnessing people? Is it (52) revelation and the continuation of the incarnation?

2. Why is it that among the four marks of the church in

Acts 2:42 (devotion to the apostles' teaching, fellowship, breaking of bread, and prayers) it is the third (Eucharist) that is designated as constitutive for the life of the church?

3. Does the church "beget" the faithful (28; 64)? Does it do this through baptism?

4. Where in the allusions to the eschatological dimension of the church (e.g., 48-50; 65) do we find the return of Christ as the judge? Where do we find the "new Jerusalem," the holy city that comes down from God out of heaven (Rev. 21:2), and does not ascend to him? Where indeed is the new creation (Teilhard de Chardin)?

5. Is the exegesis alluded to in 55-58 able to support the Mariology erected on it? Can it support the exhortation to a special cult of Mary (66)? Does this whole matter belong (as Karl Rahner asks) to the central Christian truths?

DOGMATIC CONSTITUTION
ON DIVINE REVELATION

I. QUESTIONS FOR CLARIFICATION

1. What did the Council want to avoid in rejecting the title "On the Sources of Revelation"?

2. Why does this Constitution not have a first chapter "On God," parallel to the chapter that opens and dominates the corresponding Constitution from Vatican I?

3. Why is it that in chapter I of this Constitution the knowledge of God is spoken of only at the end of the chapter (6, 2), and then not in explanation of the main statement of Vatican I but only by quoting it?

4. Why is chapter I of this Constitution opened and dominated by statements that are christological and soteriological in nature (2-6, 1)?

5. Why does this Constitution lack all the apologetical material of chapters II-IV from Vatican I ("On Faith and Reason . . .")? This happened in spite of the "pastoral" intention of Vatican II!

6. What is the reason for the appearance here of a specific teaching concerning the "transmission" (=tradition) of revelation? 10, 2ff. even speaks of a triad of tradition, Scripture, and teaching office, interpreting two of them, or all three. Why, however, does the Constitution in fact speak in chapters III-VI only of the sacred Scripture?

II. CRITICAL QUESTIONS

1. If, according to 4, 2, there is no new "public revela-

tion," and if (7f.) the tradition consists only in handing on and testifying to the revelation which the apostles received and bore witness to, and if (10, 2) the teaching office is not above the Word of God (which in 24 is equated with the Scripture!) but is in its service, then why is tradition given precedence over Scripture (7, 2; 9; 10, 1; 10, 3)? How did we get the triad of tradition, Scripture, and teaching office, and their interdependence (10, 3)? How did the *"pari pietatis affectu"* ("with the same sense of devotion") of Trent come to be included here?

2. If what is said of Scripture in 21 is valid, in what respect is participation in the Eucharist the growth (*incrementum*) of the spiritual life of the Church, while the veneration of the Word of God is only the stimulus (*impulsus*) to this life?

PASTORAL CONSTITUTION ON THE CHURCH IN THE MODERN WORLD

1. Are we justified in regarding this Constitution (at least in the light of the intention of Pope John XXIII) as the real heart of all the work of the Council?

2. How are we to understand the remarkable parallelism between the demands and promises of the Bible and Christianity and the origin, meaning, and destiny of the developments of the secular world?

3. Is it true that, especially in chapter II, the classic words of the French Revolution—Liberty, Equality, and Fraternity—are integrated in due form into Catholic social theory?

4. Do the many eschatological allusions (the strongest is found in chapter III, 39) refer to a goal that is immanent in the development of the world or to one that transcends it?

II. CRITICAL QUESTIONS

1. Does the thorough optimism of this Constitution over the possibilities of the development of the world correspond to the emphases of the Synoptic Gospels and the Letters of Paul?

2. Is it so certain that dialogue with the world is to be placed ahead of proclamation to the world?

3. Why does the Constitution set forth so few concrete positions? Where is the prophetic function of the Council in the face of the real problems of the middle of our century?

DECREE ON ECUMENISM

1. Are all (including Catholics) called on in the ecumenical dialogue:

(a) "to examine their own faithfulness to Christ's will for the Church and, wherever necessary, undertake with vigor the task of renewal and reform" (4, 2)?

(b) to make the first approaches to the separated brethren (4, 5)?

(c) but above all "to make an honest and careful appraisal of whatever needs to be renewed and achieved in the Catholic household itself" (4, 5)?

2. Is it permissible (or perhaps necessary) in the future to regard the Catholic Church as involved in "that continual reformation of which she always has need" (6, 2)?

3. What is the meaning of "an order or 'hierarchy' of truths" in Catholic teaching, which "vary in their relationship to the foundation of the Christian faith" (11, 3)? What are the "essentials" (4, 7)?

4. Are the following statements (17, 1) applicable only to the Eastern "separated brethren":

(a) the statement that "sometimes one tradition has come nearer than the other to an apt appreciation of certain aspects of a revealed mystery";

(b) the statement that "these various theological formulations are often to be considered as complementary rather than conflicting"?

II. CRITICAL QUESTIONS

1. What is the meaning of "among our separated brethren also" (1, 3), since the ecumenical movement arose outside the Catholic Church, and since Catholics are now at last called on to participate in it (4, 1; 4, 11; 24, 2)?

2. Why is this initiative of the non-Catholic churches not explicitly recognized (3, 1-4; 7ff.)?

3. Is 3, 5 intended to imply that the party of Cephas mentioned in 1 Corinthians 1:12, in distinction from the other three, was the one complete Catholic Church?

4. What is the significance for the definition of the concept "separated brethren" (lack of "fullness") of the statement (4, 10) that it is difficult for the Catholic Church herself "to express in actual life her full catholicity in all its aspects"?

5. Why is the most grievous, the fundamental schism— the opposition of Church and synagogue (Rom. 9-11; Eph. 2)—not dealt with here, but only spoken of as the relation of the Church to "Abraham's stock" in the Declaration on the Relationship of the Church to Non-Christian Religions?

DECREE ON THE APOSTOLATE
OF THE LAITY

I. QUESTIONS FOR CLARIFICATION

1. In the light of the statements about the calling of the laity (3, 1—4, 4), their "right and duty" (3, 3; 25, 1), their belonging directly to Christ, their being endowed with the Holy Spirit, with faith, hope, and love, their participation in the three offices of Christ and in the mission of the Church (2-4), and in view of the statements in 29, 2-7 about their training, what is the basic, essential difference between the apostolate of the laity and that of the whole Church?

2. Is not the apostolate of the laity the genuine form of the apostolate of the Church as such, within which there are also various functions? In what way can there be alongside the apostolate of the laity a special apostolate of the hierarchy?

3. Does the desire that the laity be active (9) include also the women mentioned in this paragraph? In 5 (and also 10, 1) this activity is to be exercised "both in the Church and in the world, in both the spiritual and the temporal orders."

4. Has the Secretariat for the Lay Apostolate already been established, and is it functioning?

II. CRITICAL QUESTIONS

1. Why is the lay apostolate not based on the definition of the Church as the "People (*laos*) of God" rather than on the reference to the needs of the times (1, 2)?

2. If Mary (4, 9) is the "perfect example" of the apostolate of the laity, and as such the "Queen of Apostles"
(and therefore of Peter and his colleagues and successors), is it not then necessary to speak of the superiority
of the apostolate of the laity to all other forms of the
apostolate of the Church?

3. Is not the concept of testimony, which is used in this
decree (11, 2; 11, 5; 13, 1, etc.) to designate the task of
the laity, a suitable designation of the task of the whole
Church in her relation to the world (Acts 1:8; 2:32,
etc.)? In 27, 1 it is stated explicitly as "the common duty
of Christian witness."

DECREE ON THE MISSIONARY ACTIVITY OF THE CHURCH

I. QUESTIONS FOR CLARIFICATION

1. How is this decree related to the Constitution on the Church, to that on the Church in the Modern World, and to the Declaration on Religious Freedom? On the basis of these other documents the reader is not prepared for the magnificent basic thesis of this decree (2, 1; 35, 1; 20, 9) according to which "the Church is missionary by her very nature," and mission is the concern of the Church because it is the Church.

2. In the development of this basic thesis should we not be reminded that the Church was always sick and could not resist the physical and intellectual force of the "world" wherever it hesitated or ceased to be a missionary church? (Asia Minor, North Africa, Eastern Balkans, Lutheran and Reformed Orthodoxy!)

3. Is not the reverse also true, that it is a criterion of the authenticity of the movements for development, renewal, and reform within the Church, whether the Church continues in a new commitment to its missionary task? (We Protestants must confess that the Reformation in the sixteenth century fell behind the Counter-Reformation—Society of Jesus—in this respect and did not set about improving at this point until the eighteenth century.)

4. Is it accidental that it is precisely in this decree (especially 1-9)

(a) that the arguments are so thoroughly and convincingly exegetical?

(b) that the role of the sacrifice of the Mass is so inconspicuous?

(c) that Mariology seems to be unnecessary in this context?

II. CRITICAL QUESTIONS

1. Again and again, is it the Church which *saves* and *renews* the world (1, 2)? Is not her task of testifying to Christ through the proclamation of the gospel between his first and his second coming, great and magnificent enough?

2. Is Catholic propaganda among newly baptized non-Catholics included in what is said in 6, 6 and 7, 2 about the call to the unity of the Church as a missionary task?

3. Or do the splendid statements in 15, 5 and 29, 5 about ecumenism even in mission lands exclude this?

DECLARATION ON THE RELATIONSHIP OF THE CHURCH TO NON-CHRISTIAN RELIGIONS

I. QUESTIONS FOR CLARIFICATION

Christians should not persecute or discriminate against their fellowmen because they are of another race or class or because of their non-Christian religion (4, 8). Rather they should treat them as brothers (5, 1) for the sake of Christ who died "because of the sins of all men, so that all might attain salvation" (4, 9) and for the sake of God "who is the Father of all" (5, 1). Because of the partial truth more or less visible in the non-Christian religions (as rays of that Truth which enlightens all men, 2, 5) these religions are to be respected as expressions of the universal longing for this truth (1, 3; 2, 1-4). Therefore Christians should cultivate dialogue and joint projects with them (2, 1; 4, 6). But the Church must never cease to proclaim Christ to them as the way, the truth, and the life, as the fullness of the religious life, as the one in whom God reconciled the world to himself (2, 5), and whose cross is a sign of God's all-embracing love (4, 9).

This is my interpretation of the declaration in its most favorable sense. Is it that of the Council?

II. CRITICAL QUESTIONS

1. Why is it so difficult (perhaps impossible) to give this document such a favorable interpretation as I have given it?

2. In what passages in the Old or New Testaments is there an analogy to the presentation and interpretation of "non-Christian religions" in the historical and analytical manner that dominates this Declaration?

3. Why is the critical and missionary task of the Church in reference to the religions as such only marginal to the Declaration and not central to it?

4. Would not the justifiable human concern of the Declaration have been expressed better by adhering to the proven methods of Paul, the apostle to the Gentiles, in which he proclaimed nothing to Jews or Greeks but the One who had been crucified for them—a stumbling block to the first and folly to the others—in order to address them as men from that point, and to call them to a realization of their common humanity?

5. On what grounds does the Declaration (2ff.) continue the distinction, long since outgrown in the study of comparative religion, between the so-called "higher religions" and the primitive religions, when the opposition of the former to the message of the cross is much more obvious and dangerous?

6. On what grounds does the Declaration (4, 1ff.) speak of the past and present history of Israel in the same breath with Hinduism, Buddhism, and Islam as a "non-Christian" religion, while

(a) the Old Testament does not present a "religion" at all but the original form of the one revelation of God

(b) and in the existence of later and contemporary Judaism (believing or unbelieving) we have the sole natural (i.e., in terms of world history) proof of God?

7. Would it not be more appropriate, in view of the anti-Semitism of the ancient, the medieval, and to a large degree the modern church, to set forth an explicit con-

fession of guilt here, rather than in respect to the separated brethren?

8. And in 3, 2 where Islam is mentioned, would not such a confession be appropriate in view of the deplorable role of the Church in the so-called Crusades?

DECLARATION ON RELIGIOUS FREEDOM

I. QUESTIONS FOR CLARIFICATION

In this Declaration the Council is not addressing Christians or the Church, but, on their behalf, is speaking to national governments (*pro domo*) (1, 3). It demands from governments the free scope due Christians and the Church for the confirmation and spreading of their faith, as the only true religion (1, 3-4; 15, 1, etc.). As the basis for this demand it cites the natural dignity of the human person (2, 2; 15, 2, etc.). This religious freedom is indirectly confirmed and made clear in revelation by the nature of faith (10) and by the relationship of Christ to his apostles (10-11) and has been basically always upheld by the Church (12). It demands this freedom as the right of every man, incidentally also for non-Catholics and their organizations, but above all as the right of Catholic Christians and the Catholic Church, to be established by juridical and legal means and consequently to be respected by civil governments. It finally points out to these governments that the fulfilling of this demand is in their own best interests (6; 8, 3; 15, 4).

Have I correctly understood and expressed the meaning and the intent of this Declaration?

II. CRITICAL QUESTIONS

1. Is it legitimate for the Church (and not only the Catholic Church) to make this demand in view of the extensive periods of her history which were dominated by her pact with the state through "*cogite intrare*"?

Would not a rather comprehensive confession of guilt be more appropriate here? Is this need met by the statement in 12, 1, "In the life of the People of God ... there have at times appeared ways of acting which were less in accord with the spirit of the gospel and even opposed to it. Nevertheless, the doctrine of the Church that no one is to be coerced into faith has always stood firm"?

2. When or where did the witnesses in the Old and New Testaments demand a legally assured scope for their life and the proclamation of their faith, and for the presentation of other religions?

3. When or where did they defend their freedom to act by reference to the natural dignity of the human person?

4. When or where did they commend this freedom to the authorities as being in their own best interests?

5. When or where did they react to the threats of oppression which the ruling powers raised against freedom in any other manner than by resisting and suffering?

6. Why does this Declaration (except for the final sentence in 15, 5) have nothing to say about the true freedom for which the Son makes us free (John 8:36), which is there where the Spirit of the Lord is present (2 Cor. 3:17), and nothing about the liberating "law of the Spirit of life in Christ Jesus" (Rom. 8:2), into which the Church continuously looks (James 1:25) and which is itself judgment (James 2:12)? In short, why does it say nothing about the "glorious liberty of the children of God" (Rom. 8:21)?

7. Could not the Church, which is called to *this* freedom (Gal. 5:13) and stands in it (Gal. 5:1), by speaking to and for itself have given more powerful testimony to governments and to all mankind about "religious freedom" than it did in this Declaration?

"CONCILIORUM TRIDENTINI ET VATICANI I INHAERENS VESTIGIIS"?

"CONCILIORUM TRIDENTINI ET VATICANI I INHAERENS VESTIGIIS"?

These words are found in the preface to the "Dogmatic Constitution on Divine Revelation," which cost the fathers of the Second Vatican Council so much concern and labor from the first session to the last. Because I wish to make them the object of certain irenically critical observations I have put a question mark after them. In Eduard Stakemeier's commentary on this Constitution (Paderborn: 1966) he translates them in context as follows: "Therefore (the Holy Synod), in the succession of the Councils of Trent and First Vatican, wishes to set forth the authentic teaching on divine revelation and its transmission" (p. 99). I cannot recall any passage in the actions of Vatican II with which I am familiar where the fathers made such specific reference to these two previous Councils. There is one exception, in the address which Pope John XXIII delivered at the opening of the first session, October 11, 1962. The Latin text is unfortunately not available to me, so I will use here the work of Mario von Galli and Bernhard Moosbrugger, *Das Konzil und Seine Folgen* (Lucerne, 1966). This is a notable book for both its texts and its pictures. On page 27 we find the following statement about the tasks the Pope was committing to the Council: "The statements handed down from the acts of the Council of Trent and the First Vatican Council must be examined and interpreted calmly and with a good conscience. In response to the demands of our own day, these teachings must be recognized, studied, and interpreted in all their fullness and depth." It must be admitted that the two decisive words in that quotation, "inhaerens vestigiis," permit the translation Stakemeier gave them, "in the succession of." They would then stress the loyalty to Trent and Vatican I in which Vatican II intended to handle the themes dealt with in those Councils. Following in their tracks, it intended to say the same thing they said.

The disadvantage of this translation is that it does not express the research, examination, and explanation of the positions of those earlier Councils which John XXIII felt to be so necessary. It looks only to the past, not to the present task of the Council of 1962-1965 which was so vigorously undertaken in this very Constitution. And it does not look at all to the future development of church doctrine. It harmonizes too much (this is to some extent true of Stakemeier's whole book), and fails to make the other element visible, the new, which, compared with those older documents, is effectively brought out in the doctrine of revelation of Vatican II. In the context of those two words it is said that the Council intends to present the genuine—Stakemeier translates, "authentic" (*echt*)—doctrine of divine revelation and its transmission. Does not this imply that the statements of those older documents, because they are not quite adequate, should not be the final word on the subject, but that they must be surpassed today by further statements, which will supplement some points and omit others?

It is not in order to remain static in its teachings (*inhaerens* can hardly be interpreted in that sense) that the Council of the twentieth century follows in the footsteps of the Councils of the sixteenth and the nineteenth centuries, but in order to fix the left foot firmly in them and then with the right foot step forward along the line they have indicated. That is, it does this in order to proceed from them and thereby make another new footprint for the Church of the future and give to the present and future another new form of her "genuine" teachings. The result is that it corresponds better with the guidelines of the first Pope of the Council to translate those words rather freely as "moving forward from the footsteps of those Councils." My interest in this question of translation will be readily understood! If this Constitution merely wished to repeat what was said at Trent and at Vatican I, if the *inhaerens* was speaking of a remaining in those footsteps, or of a "marching in place," then the very beginning of *Dei Verbum* would characterize it as a matter of little concern for us poor separated brethren. But as one of these separated brethren I would like to try to show in a few observations—I repeat, irenically critical observations—that we can say to this Constitution, and say it in its relationship to those earlier Councils, at least an honest "*Placet juxta modum,*" and to show how we can say it. I intend nothing more.

In the schema first presented to the Council the title of this Constitution was to be "On the Sources of Revelation." Following Trent (Denzinger 783) two sources of revelation would have been discussed, that is, Holy Scripture on the one hand, and tradition on the other; and following Vatican I three or even four sources (see Denzinger 1781), (1) the Scripture, (2) tradition, and in effect, (3) nature and reason which in any case make possible a sure knowledge of the one God, Creator and Lord (Denzinger 1782-1784, 1800, 1806), and finally, (4) the teaching office of the Church (Denzinger 1821 ff.). The Constitution *Dei Verbum*, however, shows in a way that cannot be overlooked that while it had these distinctions of the previous Councils in mind, and did not reject them, but applied them, or at least commemorated them in appropriate places, yet at the same time it intended to "examine and interpret them." Respect for the doctrine formulated in 1546 and 1870 produces in chapter II of our Constitution, as I will show later, a regrettable lack of clarity. But this does not obscure the things that are stated obviously. The plural "sources" (Denzinger 1787) disappeared from the title of the second schema presented to the Council, and does not reappear in the wording of the text. The title is in the plain singular, "On Divine Revelation," and the text speaks of *one revelation* (4), beside which there can be no question of any other before Christ's last revelation of himself at his return. In addition, it speaks of only *one source* of revelation. The Holy Scripture and it alone is termed the "words of God" (*locutio Dei*, 8), and "really . . . the word of God" (*vere verbum Dei*, 24) because it and it alone is the written documentation, produced by the power of the Holy Spirit ("once and for all," 21), of the divine revelation itself, described in the first chapter (9; 11). The Scriptures present directly the "Word of God Himself." Therefore they must nourish and rule Christian preaching and living. In them

> the Father who is in heaven meets His children with great love and speaks with them; and the force and power in the word of God is so great that it remains the support and energy of the Church, the strength of faith for her sons, the food of the soul, the pure and perennial source of spiritual life (21).

Therefore free access must be provided to it. The Vulgate is honored (compare what Trent said about its authenticity! [Denzinger 785]), but today we need translations into the languages of the various nations, translations from the original text, and in this work the co-operation of the separated brethren is not to be despised (22). Therefore we must have biblical scholarship (23; and end of 25). Therefore Scripture is to keep, or receive, its appropriate place in theology (it is even the soul of theology), in worship, and in religious instruction (24). Therefore the regular, thorough study of Scripture is commended to priests, deacons, and catechists, and also to all the faithful in general. "For ignorance of the Scriptures is ignorance of Christ" (25). This high evaluation of Holy Scripture in the context of the transmission of the divine revelation explains the fact (which does not seem to have impressed Stakemeier) which is so astonishing by contrast to Trent and Vatican I that, of the six chapters of this Constitution, four (16 of the 26 sections) are given over to a consistent doctrine of Holy Scripture. At the same time the reader, after reading chapter II, waits in vain for a corresponding development of tradition and the teaching office. The result is that the ten sections of the first two chapters read almost like a basic and thus indispensable introduction to the treatment of this theme. The "trend to the Bible," of which H. U. von Balthasar speaks (*Wer ist ein Christ?* 4th ed. 1966, p. 33) in view of the general development of Catholic theology and practice, is unmistakably characteristic of the highly esteemed chapters III and VI, but also of the whole Dogmatic Constitution *Dei Verbum*, approved by the Council and confirmed by the Pope. And it is also unmistakable that this trend is completely foreign to Trent and Vatican I. The footprints of those Councils lie far behind what Vatican II meant and said in this matter.

Now it is true that the clarity of these statements is

obscured in chapter II of the Constitution, which Stakemeier (*op. cit.*, p. 122) calls the "heart, midpoint, and
focus of the whole Constitution." How differently we
can read and judge! For my part I regard this second
chapter as the great fit of weakness which befell the
Council in the editing of our text. By the way in which
the holy tradition and, in 10, the teaching office of the
Church also are placed alongside the Holy Scriptures,
this chapter obscures the unmistakable declaration of
chapter I in reference to revelation itself and of chapters
III-VI in reference to Scripture, and thereby to some
extent the intent of the whole document. The tradition
hands on the revelation of God, which is once for all
uniquely documented in Scripture, to the Church of the
post-apostolic period, which was founded by Scripture,
and thus also to the Church and the world of the present
day. The authentic interpretation of Scripture is entrusted and committed to the teaching office. We separated brethren of the West will certainly not pronounce
a simple *non placet* to this differentiation of the response
to God's revelation given by men illumined by the Holy
Spirit, of which the Holy Scriptures are the first and
decisive part, and certainly not to the prominence given
to the concepts "tradition" and "teaching office." In con-
sistency with the assertion at the end of 4 that there are
no further revelations, the Constitution says expressly in
8 that the development of tradition does not involve an
accretion to revelation itself, but a growth of the
Church's understanding of the revelation. And 10, 2 says
that the "teaching office is not above the word of God,
but serves it, teaching only what has been handed on,
listening to it devoutly, guarding it scrupulously, and
explaining it faithfully by divine commission and with
the help of the Holy Spirit."

We must admit that the problems involved in the concepts "tradition" and "teaching office" exist on our side and cannot be ignored. As for the concept "tradition," did not the churches which arose in the Reformation in the sixteenth century appeal with one accord to the Councils of the first several centuries? And were we not justified in developing the traditions that became fixed in the various "confessions" (up to and including the Theological Declaration of Barmen in 1934) and also unwritten traditions? And as for the concept "teaching office," do we not have among the major Protestant churches one that even today is called not merely "Evangelical," but which, after the name of her great originator and founder, is emphatically called "Evangelical Lutheran"? And did not Calvin exercise in the sixteenth century in Geneva, in all of French-speaking Protestantism, and even far beyond, a function not entirely unlike the office of Peter in Rome?

Even without the office of Peter we have never had a total lack, nor should we ever, of charismatic figures who in their circle and for their age have represented joyously and successfully, as ones truly called, the office of faithfully interpreting the word as it was written and handed on. As a result we on our side should be cautious about protesting against the sentence in 9, which in context is very unguarded and confusing. It reads, "it is not from sacred Scripture alone that the Church draws her certainty about everything which has been revealed." We do not live, think, and teach on the basis of a Scripture that is suspended all alone in the air, and thus not "*sola*" (=*solitaria*) *Scriptura*. We live, think, and teach (don't we do it in the same way and in agreement with the previously mentioned trend of the Constitution *Dei Verbum*?) in the communion of the saints, as we listen

with filial reverence and brotherly love to the voice of
the pastors and teachers of God's people, those of the
past as well as those of the present. But first and last we
do so as we adhere to the revelation of God to which
the Holy Scriptures bear witness, which is inspired by
the Holy Spirit, and which gives inspiration; that is, we
do so in obeying in faith the living voice of Jesus Christ.

Unfortunately we can agree with this position only
with reservations which the Council could by no means
have approved, because in chapter II as a whole it remains in the "footsteps" of Trent, or even wishes to
make them deeper. What are we to think when we read
in section 9 that *both* (tradition and Scripture) flow
"from the same divine wellspring"? What are we to
think when at the end of this section the most question-
able statement of Trent is repeated verbatim? "Both
sacred tradition and sacred Scripture are to be accepted
and venerated with the same sense of devotion and reverence." What does it mean to say "both"? Doesn't this
mean speaking again of two, or even three (in view of
what is said in 10 about the teaching office) separate, although related, sources of revelation? What does it mean
when no fewer than four times the order Scripture-
tradition is reversed (7; 9; 10)? What does it mean when
section 8 says that Scripture is made known, is understood, and is made active, not through the Holy Spirit,
by whom it was inspired, but through tradition? Does
this not mean that the relationship of the Church and of
the faithful to tradition and to Scripture is made one and
the same, following in the footsteps of Trent?

But why should they be the same? What is the meaning of "with the same sense of devotion and reverence"?
Was it not right for the Constitution *Dei Verbum* to begin in the preface by appealing to Scripture and not to

any tradition or to the teaching office? By what right does this chapter II direct the Catholic Church and the Catholic Christian to hold in the same manner to the Evangelist Matthew and to Thomas a Kempis or Ignatius Loyola as the interpreters of the Evangelists? Or the Protestant Church or a Protestant Christian to give the same respect to the Apostle Paul and to Luther or Calvin, or perhaps to Zinzendorf or Blumhardt? Is not such an undifferentiated equating of Scripture and tradition unjustifiable in both cases? Is it not mandatory to distinguish fundamentally between the respect and the love accorded there to a sainted teacher of the Church or to the "Holy Father" in Rome and here to a charismatic theologian or churchman on the one hand, and on the other, the obedience of faith with which we are to heed, both here and there, the witness of the biblical prophets and apostles to revelation? The painful weakness of chapter II of this Constitution is that this distinction is not only not commended, but in continuity with Trent is actually excluded.

What basis or justification is there for carrying this out in view of all that is so splendidly said in chapter VI about the Scripture in the life of the Church? In short, the darkness of this chapter is considerable, in contrast to the general tendency of the Constitution. It is all the more considerable in that *Dei Verbum* could be a helpful model for us others in dealing with the problems of "tradition" and "teaching office" which we tend to neglect. At this point there is much to be done in what Pope John XXIII commended as "testing and interpreting," especially the heritage of Trent. And we others are also called on to participate.

It should be said, however, that the attack of weakness

which befell the Council in chapter II in its relationship
to the two preceding Councils, especially that of Trent,
is more than made up for by the strength of the material
presented so freely in what precedes and in what follows
this dismal chapter. In this connection I want to cite one
more example of the way in which the material we are
considering here is related to Vatican I. Keep in mind the
content and methods of the "Dogmatic Constitution on
the Catholic Faith" of 1870 (Denzinger 1781 ff.) and
chapter I, "Revelation Itself," of 1965. In the former,
despite the title of this Constitution which deals with the
faith, there is literally no word at all in any of the four
chapters about the origin, object, and content of the
Catholic faith, not even in chapter II, entitled "On Revelation," or in chapter III, "On Faith." In the latter document, however, the preface plunges into the middle of
the question. The Council is not debating about the
Catholic faith, it is proclaiming it. It hears and proclaims
God's word in appealing to what is written in 1 John 1—
the eternal life which appeared to the apostles, which
they saw, which they touched, which was made known
to them in order to establish their fellowship with those
whom they are addressing, a fellowship identical with
what they have with the Father and with his Son Jesus
Christ.

On the same plane and in the same sense articles 2-4
continue in the chapter "Revelation Itself," of which the
Council proceeded to speak by citing a whole list of
scriptural passages. In his incarnate Word God chose to
reveal, manifest, and bear witness to himself and "out of
the abundance of His love speaks to men as friends" (2).
This "history of salvation" was realized in the deeds and
words which reveal God in the Old Testament by way
of preparation and in the New as fulfillment. God reveals

himself by being with us in Jesus Christ "to free us from the darkness of sin and death, and to raise us up to life eternal" (4). It is this (5) that is the foundation, object, and content of the Catholic "obedience of faith," which, as man's free submission, is made possible and brought about solely through the grace of the Holy Spirit.

Now, on the other hand, where in the documents of Vatican II is there a natural theology or an anathema against those who reject it? Where are all the apologetics? All the concern over the relationship of faith to reason, of nature to the supernatural, etc., which occupied the fathers of Vatican I exclusively does not seem to exist any longer for the fathers of Vatican II. It should also be noted that the formal thought patterns so characteristic of the Council of 1870 have given way to strictly objective, theological patterns, just as the earlier static views have given way to dynamic views inspired and governed by Scripture. It should also be noted how the broadly developed statements of Vatican I are reduced in Vatican II to a bare minimum, contained in two references (6). This is enough to show that God, while not absolutely and in principle inaccessible to human reason, still can really and practically be known to man only in his self-revelation, which is described in unequivocal terms in 2-5. The question whether the Council has remained true in its other documents to what is said here, and if so, to what degree, is another question, and one into which we cannot go here. When we look at the "Decree on Religious Liberty," the content of which is so important, we must certainly answer the question in the negative, unfortunately. But here the Council has certainly moved beyond the footsteps of Vatican I and in contrast to it said something which is different and new in content and method, something of which we

must never lose sight in our evaluation of the Council's
teaching about God's revelation and which is also a criterion for judging its other pronouncements.

In summary, the relationship of *Dei Verbum* to the
teachings of the two preceding Councils is essentially not
one of pointing back to them but of pointing forward
from them. Important changes, even innovations, made
from them show that the trend of the Constitution was
in the direction of a doctrine which carefully (more
carefully than we do) considers and includes the genuine
problems of "tradition" and the "teaching office," a doctrine not of the *sole* authority but of the *supreme* authority of Holy Scripture for the Church and theology.
What I termed the "attack of weakness" in chapter II
obscures this trend. This obscuring was undoubtedly the
price the Council had to pay for those changes and innovations, for the achievement of such overwhelming
agreement to the decisions of the Council, and for their
confirmation by Pope Paul VI. Complete clarity of for-
mulation was thus not attained, nor could it be expected.
Even the great charismatic figure John XXIII probably
did not expect the Council he called to convene in 1962
to produce a more thorough examination and interpretation of the work of past Councils.

The mills of God grind slow, within and without the
walls. Still, we may say that a clarity that should be
neither overlooked nor underestimated was achieved in
the preface, in chapters I and III-VI (except for minor
difficulties and lapses which I prefer not to mention
here), and thus in the whole document. This encourages
us to look to a still better future, and because of the
importance of the themes treated in this document this is
significant enough that we can say of the Second Vati-

can Council, which has now become history, that whatever else it may have been, it was a reforming Council.

What would it be like if the Council of the Twenty-first Century were to move in its Constitutions, Decrees, and Declarations "in the footsteps of the Second Council of Orange"?

A LETTER
ABOUT MARIOLOGY

A LETTER ABOUT MARIOLOGY

Basel, Oct. 21, 1966

My dear Colleague:

Shortly after my return from Rome your lecture on Mariology arrived also in good condition, and I plunged into reading it almost immediately with the same attentiveness with which I read detective stories in earlier decades, and read it through from start to finish.

Let me begin by saying the good things which I can say with a clear conscience. Your work is a powerful witness to the systematic ability, force, and skill of the author. Anyone who knows how to deal with a theme, whatever my own relation is to this one, so precisely, logically, and comprehensively in both method and content as you are obviously able to do, is assured of my respect from the outset. I was pleased also with your careful and dignified treatment of your relation to earlier and later Mariologies, and with the honesty with which you always conceded what had to be conceded in relation to the "historical" problems. Especially toward the end of your work I found more than one sentence beside which, when I ignored the context in which it was found, I could not keep from writing "Good" in the margin, like a schoolteacher. As for the content, I naturally noted with pleasure what effort you expended to relate the whole to the christological center from which your theme took its departure—I should say, and departed a long, long way.

So far so good, if, that is, Mariology as such could really be a legitimate theme of theology. If I were able to accept it as such I would then certainly register my alarm over the way in which you throughout bring together and separate the concepts "history" and "faith." By so doing you are traveling down (in Rome also I noted that you are not the only young Catholic theologian of our day to do so) the steep path to Schleiermacher and Bultmann, where you cannot in the end expect to harvest good fruit either in your theme, which is one I cannot myself accept, or in the treatment of other, genuine theological problems.

My dear colleague, you want my thorough criticism. How can I give it when I am still obliged as before to reject your presupposition as such, the possibility, justification, and necessity of Mariology? You know as well as I do, and admit it at the start, that the "theotokos" of the Council of Ephesus (and also the normal sense of the term before that) was a formula to aid in expressing Christology, and not a mariological statement, nor the enunciation of an independent dogma besides the one which the Council stated as the doctrine of the "two natures" of Christ. When this "theotokos" was used to build a Mariology—I must say here, misused—it became, however unobjectionable it was and is in itself, the starting point of a development which I can only regard as grotesque. You yourself describe it as in subsequent ages so overgrown for long stretches that it threatened the vine by which it lived, that is, the work and word of God in Jesus Christ.

Not even all the diligent reminders that it was really praise of her Son could alter the fact that the handmaid of the Lord of Luke 1 became the wearer of her own crown, to which new pearls were always being added with justification and by necessity, down to those added by Pius XII in 1950 and by Paul VI during the Second Vatican Council. It appears to me that the Church, or the Church's theology, deprived this handmaid of her best possession by making her a queen, the "queen of heaven," in unavoidable competition with "our Father who art in heaven." And it seems to me that the more this strangely contrived and decorated figure became the object of "dulia" or "hyperdulia" in the world of higher and lower piety, and the more the teaching office of the Church, as in 1854 and 1950, could appeal to the "concensus of the Church" as a form of divine revelation, the more complicated, unnatural, and difficult it became for the theologians to make the best of it. They had to provide a basis for and explain retroactively the attributes and abilities of that figure officially recognized by the Church, marking the limits against the misunderstandings that were so easy, and in the best of cases (such as your lecture) striving to make clear the relationship to God's central activity and revelation.

Pardon me for saying so, but even your Mariology, for all its honesty, which I would not deny, and precisely in the technical perfection which I admire so much, makes the impression that you were driven by no "necessity" (1 Cor. 9:16) in its production except the fact of the now existing ecclesiastical validity of the four (as you count them) dogmas of Mariology. It makes the impression that not only our mutual friend ————, but you as well find yourself genuinely perplexed in this matter. In the simplicity of a faith that is sure of its object the scholarly dogmatician can and must speak differently, that is, with less worry and caution, and therefore more confidently than you do here.

Our friend ———— whom I just mentioned, avoids, as

you know, Mariology as much as possible, and probably
has a clearer notion of the fact that it is under sentence
of death and therefore is already decayed. I will be bold
enough to prophesy that you will not deliver this lecture
again, as interesting as it is. It was no accident that while
Vatican II often acknowledged Mariology out of a sense
of duty, it deliberately avoided it in all the important
statements, or used it only for decorative purposes. I
had a similar impression when I listened to my colleagues
———— and ———— discuss their (not quite identical) mariological views in Rome. The Catholic Church does not
stand or fall (thank God) on its Mariology. And neither do you, my dear colleague.

> With warmest greetings,
> Karl Barth

APPENDIX

Thoughts on the
Second Vatican Council
by
Karl Barth
1963

THOUGHTS ON THE
SECOND VATICAN COUNCIL

My friend Dr. W. A. Visser 't Hooft has requested
that I express publicly some of the thoughts which I
presented to him in a personal conversation. I had con-
fessed to him that, in view of the remarks (so far as I
knew of them) which he and his circle in Geneva had
made regarding the Council, I could not find anything
to contradict and yet could not be altogether satisfied.
Even after reading the fine lecture by Lukas Vischer on
"Community of the Separated Churches?" (in the
"Polis"-booklet *Zwischen zwei Konzilssessionen*, Evan-
gelischer Verlag, Zürich), I am not completely reassured.

If I have read and understood correctly, the interest of
the Geneva central office of non-Roman ecumenicism
has up to the present centered on the question whether,
to what extent, and in what form the result of the Council might lead to closer attention and greater receptivity
on the part of the Roman Church for the rest of Christianity, and on this basis to new and more frequent contact
and conversations, to a dialogue between Rome and the
rest of us. This is certainly a legitimate and important
question, which Pope John XXIII himself has actually
stimulated by his wish (carried out against certain circles
of his Church) to invite "observers" from the ranks of
the World Council and some of the larger non-Roman
churches. At a special reception in the Vatican he osten-
tatiously placed himself in the midst of these observers.
They were supplied with the confidential literary ma-

terial which was otherwise available only to the actual participants in the Council. They were constantly addressed in St. Peter's Cathedral as the *dilectissimi observatores*. Behind the scenes and privately, individually and in groups, they were evidently greeted, consulted, and requested to express their views on the themes that were treated. What innovations! Certainly there has been a very remarkable beginning here of contacts between the teaching office of the Roman Church and representatives of the other confessions which are not subordinated to it and nevertheless have the intention also of being "catholic," with the result that the question about the continuation of such contacts is sensible and definitely worthwhile. However, for two reasons it seems to me not quite right to observe and judge the event of the Council primarily (not to say exclusively) from this one aspect.

Is there not in this way an underestimation of the significance which this no doubt important question has in the Roman Church itself? Our own side has realized and often stressed the fact that the Council is an affair of this Church itself. Perhaps, however, this fact has not been accepted definitely enough. The task of the Council is the Church's *own inner renewal*, to be carried out in view of its present Christian and non-Christian environment. Its ultimate goal (stressed sharply enough in the first announcements of the Pope) is the development of its own splendor, a development that is in a certain sense kerygmatic, contemporary, inviting the Christian and non-Christian environment to peace, even to union with the Church itself. Obviously, to achieve this goal the Church must be interested in gaining a full and accurate picture of its *immediate* or *Christian* environment, and in giving this also a clear picture of itself. But *this* intention (although not one that had become so evident in its previous history) was the basis for founding this astonishing relationship with the other churches—concretely, in the special activity of Cardinal Bea and his co-workers. And the intention would still be *this* one should this relationship be continued, perhaps even deepened and strengthened, after the Council itself. As far as we others are concerned, the Council was called not in order to negotiate with us but in order to get to know us better and explain to us the true essence of the Roman Church, and in this way to impress us (in the best sense of the word). And matters will remain the same in all the developments that follow the Council. Is this fact not overlooked if someone should think that the Roman Church has an *independent*, a *primary* interest in the initiation and cultivation of those contacts? Are we well advised, therefore, to direct our interest in the Council all too intensively or even exclusively to those conversational contacts which have newly arisen and may perhaps be expanded, or to concentrate the question about certain communications that have arisen out of these contacts in the single question whether Rome is or may become willing to learn this thing or the other from us? (Such accents have already been sounded.) This is not to overlook or deny the fact that Rome may inconspicuously have learned from us and will continue to do so. The Church (and also the non-Roman Church) has always done well to learn (and to learn more than a little) from its heretics and schismatics. But still less can we overlook the fact (if we do not wish to bypass altogether the thought of our best Roman negotiators) that the papal *and* the conciliar Rome is today concerned centrally and actually with the renovation of its own house, and that only for this reason, peripherally and contingently, is it

concerned to hear and accept us as its discussion partners.
(This very fact could also be positively significant and
exemplary for us.) This is the first reservation which
I wish to mention here: our concentration on the question of present and future contacts and communication
between Rome and ourselves seems to me to lack a
certain sober realism with respect to the "ecumenical"
purpose (precisely in *Rome's* sense) which guides Rome
in its Council.

My second reservation extends further and deeper.
The concentration on that question seems to me to be
too formal to be altogether realistic. It was certainly
saying a bit too much when an enthusiastic Roman cor-
respondent of the *Süddeutsche Zeitung* spoke of a "truly
temperamental blowing of the Holy Spirit" under whose
auspices the first session of the Council took place. But
we others, no doubt, are not only allowed but even re-
quired to realize that both the convocation and the previous course of the Council are symptomatic of a certain
landslide that is taking place in the Roman Church, a
spiritual movement actually taking place there, with
whose possibility no one had reckoned fifty years ago.
This movement was what demanded something like a
renovation and a second Vatican Council. It expresses
itself in the previous events of the Council. My question
is whether it is not more important and imperative for
us of "another faith" to direct our attention and con-
troversy to it, instead of being so formally concerned
with future contacts.

What is involved here? May not the old book of the
Gospels which during the opening of the Council was
laid in the direct line of vision of the bishops (and observers!) in St. Peter's Cathedral have been more than
just a necessary piece of liturgical and ornamental scen-

ery? What that very remarkable man Angelo Roncalli as Pope John XXIII undertook in this matter and in bringing the bishops together, what the tenor of the opening address of the Pope displayed, what the majority of the Council characteristically was motivated by in the previous course of its proceedings: was all this not the dynamics of the beginning of a reorganization—precisely around the gospel? The Bible of the Old and New Testaments was obviously for a long time past read more industriously and fruitfully in clerical (and not only in clerical) circles of the Roman Church than we had noticed or properly judged. (This was clearly expressed in the discussion and preliminary decision concerning "Scripture and Tradition.") Were we staring all too fixedly, perhaps, at the problematic formulas of Trent or the spectacular sorrows of those Catholic theologians who were laboring at scientific exegesis? Had we not put enough trust in the leavening power of the Word of Scripture, which after all is strongly represented in the Roman book of the Mass and the breviary? Were we confused by all the strange elements that encountered us there? And, through this presence of the prophetic and apostolic Scriptures, has not Jesus Christ inevitably stepped anew into the center of faith of the Roman Christians and the thought of the Roman theologians— just at the place where he seemed increasingly called in question by the discouraging development of the dogmas about Mary? And as a result, have not surprising interpretations been offered of the questions which interested the sixteenth century concerning the relationship between divine and human freedom or between faith and its works—interpretations which explain in a remarkable way or even surpass the Tridentine doctrine of justification and also the doctrine of reason and revela-

tion presented in the first Vatican Council? Can it be
overlooked, furthermore, that the preaching in the Roman congregations is not only more industrious but also
much more serious than our previous ideas would allow,
and that in this matter there are often considerable sur-
prises to be experienced—for instance, on the radio—in
comparison with many Protestant presentations? More-
over, has not a movement begun (extending even to the
architecture of the churches) in the direction of a more
active participation of the congregation in the altar service, which takes place no longer by a distant wall but
in its midst, giving it its character as a worship service?
This is the fact (with regard to the active hearing of
the word of God) which has become clear in the discussions of the Council concerning reform of the liturgy.
Does not this movement spur us to closer attention and
reconsideration, astonished as we were by the sacerdotal
remarkableness of this altar service and its interpretations
that were previously presented and heard? Certainly
there is no occasion for overestimating in any dimension
the spiritual event which is tentatively announced by
all this, and there is reason to be prepared for every
possible sort of roadblock and reversal. Everything is
still very imperfect and very unclear to us, both in par-
ticulars and as a whole, and things may remain this way
for a long time, perhaps to the second coming of Christ.
There is no reason for anyone to dream that the Roman
Catholics might become "evangelical" in *our* sense,
whether tomorrow, the day after tomorrow, or at any
other time. The very fact that this movement began altogether in the *Roman* Catholic sphere, in the form of
its theoretical and practical decrees, leading nonetheless
to certain explosions in the present Council at the real
or supposed grave of Peter, explosions which will not

be so easy to do away with—this fact itself could give
to the movement its greatest significance for us.

Of course, that mariological dogma with its so disa-
greeable development is still in existence, with its un-
canny relationship to the essence and function of the
Church. The present Pope apparently does not intend
to take further steps in its development. But there is also
no question of even its partial revocation. At the beginning of everything, beclouding everything, stands the
dogma summarized and proclaimed in the first Vatican
Council concerning the prolongation of the office of
Peter in each bearer of the papal crown and the infalli-
bility of his judgment in matters of doctrine and life
when he speaks *ex cathedra* (with or without the agreement of the other bishops or the rest of the Church
altogether). And round about his throne are those invisi-
ble principalities and powers which are called the "Curia,"
holding forth inscrutably through their varied interplay
of forces. As to those dogmas, however, it may be noted
that there is a flexibility, highly developed in recent
Roman Christianity and ecclesiasticism and especially in
recent Roman theology, with regard to the stress or lack
of stress laid on the different decisions that were made
in earlier times. There is also a remarkable proficiency
in interpreting these subsequently *in meliorem* or even
in optimam partem, that is to say, as "evangelical"
(within the limits of their special ecclesiastical character).
Let us wait and see whether these attempts will succeed,
whether those biggest roadblocks which have not yet
been noticeably touched by the movement that mani-
fested itself in the Council will be subsequently presented to us in a clear and understandable form, in which
they would appear somewhat more harmless and less
worthy of our wrath than they now appear to us, even

though we might still be unable to pass them unhindered. Is it altogether insignificant that the one occasion upon which John XXIII made use of his singular authority during the previous course of the Council was the reception of St. Joseph into the canon of the Mass—the biblical figure, therefore, whose special character in relation to the son of Mary can be found only in his constant and unambiguous role as a *witness*? What is the Church if this witness is her "protector," as he has been named for a long time past? Certainly she is then not the image of a gleaming Mother of God and Queen of Heaven but instead the image of that altogether human "guardian father" who is easily overlooked because his relationship to the chief character is precisely that of a *servant*. Naturally I do not even dream of maintaining that this is what the Pope *intended* to say with his unexpected emphasis on Joseph. I only wish to note that in this way he actually ("infallibly"?) *did* say something that points in this direction. Likewise the principalities and powers of the "Curia" have in fact already proven not to be altogether dominant in the previous course of the Council. One member of this circle reportedly has already spoken of its "martyrdom"!

My point in all this is to suggest that we should direct our attention far more to what is beginning to appear as a movement of renewal *within* the Roman Church, to what in fact has already been partially set in motion, rather than to the possibilities of a loyal correspondence between us and its representatives. In the last analysis, Rome and the non-Roman churches are not static power groups, buttressed and delimited within themselves and devoted to the preservation of their possessions or the multiplication of their prestige and influence. Both are directed to the unification of all Christianity as their final end. Both live by the dynamics of the evangelical Word and Spirit which are totally constitutive for both. Both live to the extent that they are living communities of the living Jesus Christ. The question that confronts them, first and last, each in its own way and both in their co-existence, is not the co-operation of their different doctrines and institutions but this dynamic movement. They are summoned to give mutual attention to *this* movement. And the present situation could be determined by the fact that for a change we *non-Roman* Christians are in a special way the ones who are *questioned*. Certainly, we are not asked whether we could, should, or would wish to become "Catholic," but we are asked whether, in view of the spiritual motion that is taking place there, something has been set in motion—or not set in motion! —on *our* side, in the rooms of *our* church. In view of the certainly imperfect movement over there, do we think, speak, and act in a movement of *our own,* similar in all its imperfection—a movement that consists not only in the preservation of the oft-cited "heritage of the Reformation," not only in the cultivation of our own customs and traditions, not only (as though everything on our side were basically in good shape!) in all sorts of contemporary controversies, concerns, corrections, and new beginnings, but also in the experience and fructification of a shaking of the foundations? Do we have any idea (for instance, in the so doughty churches of the United States, but no less in the churches this side of the Atlantic) what such a fundamental crisis would be and what it could entail? Was it such a crisis that brought together, for example, the conference of New Delhi (which in itself is certainly to be taken very seriously)? Is such a thing possible at all in Eastern Orthodoxy? And do we in the European West actually exist as *eccles-*

iae semper reformandae? Or are there not among us all too many offensive movements that have made no progress—for instance, in the Evangelical Church in Germany and its spiritual paralysis that began such a short time after the brief awakening during the time of the church struggle—so that now the "progressive" elements (in contrast to the situation in St. Peter's!) form a minority with its back to the wall? Do not we non-Roman theologians lack too much that interesting and progressive flexibility which characterizes many of our Roman colleagues, interesting because it does not exclude but includes an ultimate responsibility and clear direction? Does there not exist among us an express enmity against all genuinely disturbing factors? And as a complement to this, is there not far too great a measure of conformism with respect to the powers that rule in the people, state, and society? What can be said to the fact that in Denmark, Grundtvig has become far and away more influential than Kierkegaard? Or what about the fact that American Christianity seems inwardly incapable of measuring up to the problem of integration which is so pressing there? Or what about the fact that the brave statement of the Dutch General Synod on the question of nuclear armament, instead of becoming the statement of all our churches, remains isolated as a gratifying exception? And what about the feeble evasion, on the part of the governing body of the Swiss Union of Churches, of the problem of the military chaplain who was disciplined precisely on account of his standpoint on this question? Or would anyone pretend to deduce examples to the contrary from the yearly gatherings of the churches (*Kirchentage*), the Evangelical Academies, the skirmishes about demythologizing, hermeneutics, and that sort of thing? Are there not also non-Roman, even

"Protestant," Ottavianis (small and large, confessional and liberal, episcopal and presbyterial-synodal, eternally optimistic or eternally tragic)? And are not these the ones who everywhere to some extent determine the appearance of the non-Roman churches? But if this is the case, on what topic and in what language do we propose to continue those discussions which have been hoped for with the Roman Catholics?

I freely confess that I am secretly troubled by one problem, which I cannot admit is overcome by the counter-criticism (though this lies close to hand and is certainly possible) that the "spiritual event" over there which first led to the Second Vatican Council has no solid basis. How would things look if Rome (without ceasing to be Rome) were one day simply to overtake us and place us in the shadows, so far as the renewing of the church through the Word and Spirit of the gospel is concerned? What if we should discover that the last are first and the first last, that the voice of the Good Shepherd should find a clearer echo over there than among us? I once asked Hans Küng whether he would repeat *viva voce* what he has presented in his book on justification, if one fine day he were to become the Roman Pope (which of course is not an excluded possibility). "Of course!" was his immediate and undaunted reply, to which I could only say that then I really stood in fear and trembling for Protestantism, in whose ranks the theses of his Catholic book had by no means gained common acceptance, and which would therefore have to submit to being set right (in this admittedly extreme case) from the throne of Peter, and that in a matter of its own most intimate concern. Hans Küng's reply was: "And that will happen, too!" Whether "that" will happen is a question we may put to one side. But it could

very well be possible that we others might find more
to learn from the Roman Church than Rome for its part
would have to learn from us, as we still assume with
undue self-satisfaction. (We would learn, of course, not
from its special doctrine, liturgy, and other institutions
but from a new Spirit that revitalizes and sets these dead
bones in motion.) Certainly, many proper and important
things have already been said (fortunately, some things
that were also offensive for certain ears) at Amsterdam,
Evanston, and New Delhi—and not first in the Easter
Encyclical of John XXIII—about human rights, the
problems of race, minorities, refugees, and colonialism,
the task of the United Nations, atomic and general dis-
armament. But why is it that the voice of Rome made
a far greater impression than the voice of Geneva on
the world (from the editor's desk of *Pravda* all the way
to that of the *Basler Nationalzeitung*)? Was it only because of the obviously greater historical and political
halo which Rome possesses? Is not the reason also the
fact that in the encyclical the same things were not only
talked about but also *proclaimed*, that Christianity and
the world were not only taught but also *summoned*
unreservedly and bindingly with an appeal to the highest authority, that they received not only advice and
admonition but also *directives*—in short, that the encyclical had more the character of a *message* than our
previous ecumenical proclamations, in spite of its extensive use of terms and concepts taken from natural law?
I think that our side, lacking this degree of natural law,
could actually speak in this manner much more clearly.
But at the present I do not yet see that we have done so.
And therefore I am afraid that with respect to the ex-
ternal world, precisely in this decisive present of ours,
we might be left far behind by a papal church that is

making dynamic recovery. Will we also have to witness Rome's achievement of a Christian standpoint on the East-West conflict, one which is freer and more productive of world peace, *before* we achieve this? I do not wish to overestimate this encyclical, and therefore I do not say that things have gone so far already. But I think that a thoroughgoing reconsideration is called for by the very fact that the *threat* of an exchange of positions and roles is becoming visible today all along the horizon, an exchange in whose light our criticisms, justified as they are, of Mary and the infallible teaching office would necessarily become uninteresting. And this is the question which I with all respect would like to see the executive body of the World Council of Churches more diligently concerned with. Might it not be a sound Christian rule to attribute a little more worth to others than to oneself and to be a bit more critical of oneself than of others? Must not the Council (or rather what can be perceived on the Roman side in the background of the Council) give us occasion to sweep away the dust before the door of our own church with a careful but nevertheless mighty broom?

I can also formulate the question another way: should our prayer for the growing visibility of the unity of the Church of Jesus Christ not become, for our part (regardless of what may be meant in the prayer of the other side), quite freed from the thought that the brethren who are separated from us might become "evangelical" in our sense and style, and that they might sooner or later be granted an insight (treading further along the obviously good way they have begun) into the greater propriety and importance of our form of the Christian faith, the faith that is common to them and to us? Should not our prayer in this matter express the

quite firm wish that, in view of what seems to be beginning to stir over there as spiritual renewal (independently
of the question concerning the depth and future of that
renewal), something new might occur *among us*—a new
attentiveness to the Word of God *among us*, in relationship to *our* form of Christian faith or its many forms
that are included in our ecumenical movement—a new
outpouring of the Holy Spirit (to speak with J. Chr.
Blumhardt) *among us*? What help would all the prayers
about the unity of the Church be to us as long as their
central meaning was not the entreaty *Veni, creator
Spiritus*? And what help would this entreaty be to us if
we were to pray with a side glance toward those others
instead of with our gaze firmly fixed on *our* churches,
on our life in the sphere of *our* church orders, on *our*
teaching, theologizing, preaching, and instructing in the
sphere of *our* knowledge and church confessions, on
the bitter misery of *our* whole existence as a church?

Let us turn once again to the beginning of this essay.
Of what use would any conversation with those others
be to us, and how could they be conducted with a view
to a this-worldly or at least other-worldly unity of the
Church, if the presupposition on our side were something else than the altogether concrete entreaty for the
Holy Spirit within *our* troubled church? Once again,
what humiliations could befall us in such conversations if
it should prove to be the case that the participants on
the other side were in this matter more seriously en-
gaged, that the *Veni creator Spiritus* were present with
them in a more concrete directedness, and that they
were praying not in view of our own misery but with
their gaze on their *own* Roman Church problems? From
the one standpoint as from the other, the way to unity
of the Church can only be the way of her renewal. But

THE POINT

renewal means repentance. And repentance means turning about: not the turning of those others, but one's *own* turning. Is not the problem posed for the World Council of Churches by the Roman Council one of repentance and so of renewal of *our* churches, of all the non-Roman churches assembled in the World Council? And is not the continuation of our conversations with the others a secondary problem dominated by that primary one? This is the question (directed not last of all also to our "observers") which seems to me to be the *burning* question with respect to the conclusion of the Council and, in fact, far beyond this.